4-2-02

W9-CKI-763

ROUND LAKE AREA
LIBRARY
906 HART ROAD
ROUND LAKE, IL 60073
(847) 546-7060

DEMCO

THAILAND

A TRUE BOOK

by
David Petersen

Children's Press®
A Division of Scholastic Inc.

New York Toronto London Auckland Sydney
Mexico City New Delhi Hong Kong
Danbury, Connecticut

ROUND LAKE
AREA LIBRARY

Giant statues at the Grand Palace in Bangkok

Content Consultant
Kathleen Gillogly
Consulting Anthropologist

Reading Consultant
Nanci R. Vargus
Ed.D., Primary Multiage Teacher, Decatur Township Schools, Indianapolis, IN

The photograph on the cover shows Buddhist monks standing by Wat Po in Bangkok. The photograph on the title page shows children at the Chiang Mai Flower Festival.

Library of Congress Cataloging-in-Publication Data

Petersen, David, 1946-
   Thailand / by David Petersen.
      p. cm. — (True book)
   Includes bibliographical references and index.
   ISBN 0-516-22258-9 (lib. bdg.)   0-516-27361-2 (pbk.)
   1. Thailand—Juvenile literature. [1. Thailand.] 1. Title. II. Series.

DS563.5 .P45 2001
959.3—dc21   00-057026

©2001 Children's Press®
A Division of Scholastic Inc.
All rights reserved. Published simultaneously in Canada.
Printed in the United States of America.
1 2 3 4 5 6 7 8 9 10 R 10 09 08 07 06 05 04 03 02 01

Contents

Thailand is a lush,
beautiful country.

The Land of Smiles

Thailand, in Southeast Asia, is an exciting and beautiful country. Much of its beauty comes from the land itself. It has green rain forests and mountain woods, golden fields of ripening rice, bright white beaches, and turquoise seawater.

Classical Thai dancers

Thai culture is just as striking as the country's scenery. Traditional Thai costumes of orange, red, and gold glitter like ornaments. In Thailand, even the elephants are colorfully dressed!

The Thai people are known for their friendliness and hospitality to strangers. In fact, Thailand is sometimes called The Land of Smiles.

A fruit trader in a Bangkok floating market

Elephant Country

The elephant is Thailand's largest animal and an important part of its culture. With a little imagination, you can even see an elephant in Thailand's geographical shape.

This map-elephant is sitting down, with its back to the east, pressing against Laos.

The elephant's ears stick straight up into Myanmar. Its front legs dangle down, touching Cambodia on the east and the Gulf of Thailand below.

Finally, our map-elephant's long, lumpy trunk is Thailand's Southern Peninsula—a narrow strip of land separating the Gulf of Thailand from the Andaman Sea. At the end of its trunk, Thailand meets Malaysia.

Thailand is about twice as big as Wyoming. Its land is divided into four natural regions.

Phang Nga Bay on Thailand's Southern Peninsula (above); a mountainous area in the Chiang Dao district of northwest Thailand (right)

The North is mountainous, crowned by Thailand's highest peak, Doi Inthanon. It rises 8,514 feet (2,595 meters) above sea level. The Northeast

A rice field in the Central Plain (left) and a beach in southern Thailand (below)

is plateau country—high and mostly flat.

The Central Plain is an area of rich farmland that makes Thailand the world's largest exporter of rice. Traditionally, that rice was tended with water buffalo. Today most of it is tended with small, hand-held tractors called "iron buffaloes." Thailand's most important river, the Chao Phraya, runs through this region.

Thailand's Southern Peninsula has lush rain forests, perfect beaches, and offshore islands begging to be explored.

Northern Thailand is higher and cooler than the south, but most of Thailand is semi-tropical. Thailand has three seasons: hot (March-April), wet (May-October), and cool (November-February).

Bangkok (above) lies along the Chao Phraya, Thailand's most important river. A floating market in Bangkok (right)

Thailand's capital is Bangkok. As the country's largest city, this modern seaport sprawls over 600 square miles (1,554 square kilometers). Bangkok is home to nearly 6 million people.

Land of the Free

Before 1939, Thailand was called Siam. The word *Thailand* means "Land of the Free." It's a good name for this nation, since Thailand is the only Southeast Asian country that has never been controlled by a foreign power.

The Kingdom of Siam has existed for nearly eight centuries. The

Thai farmers

people who came to be known
as the Thai (the "free") came
here from China about 1,350
years ago.

Today, Thailand is home to
some 60 million people. About
three-fourths of them are Thai.
The largest minority are
Chinese, with smaller numbers

The Akha (left), Yao (below), and Lisu (bottom right) are among the mountain minorities of northern Thailand. Muslims, the largest religious minority in Thailand (bottom left), live mainly in southernmost Thailand.

of Malaysians, Indians, Laotians, Burmese, Khmer, Mon, and six different mountain minorities.

Thai is the official language, with many regional dialects. Among the well educated, English is a popular second language.

By Western standards, most Thai people live simply. Yet compared to its neighbors, Thailand is a wealthy country. More than 93 percent of its people can read and write, and unemployment is low.

Thai schoolchildren on field trip in Bangkok

After nine years of public schooling, some Thai students go on to college. Others find jobs in the tourist trade, or in government, manufacturing, or

Although some Thai people work in manufacturing (top) or mining (bottom right), most make their living by farming or fishing (bottom left).

Gardens at a Meo hill tribe village in northern Thailand

mining. But most Thai people still make their living in traditional ways—farming or fishing. Eight of every ten Thai people live in small villages rather than in the noisy cities.

From Kings to Constitutions

Thailand's government is a constitutional monarchy. "Monarchy" means rule by a royal family. Generation after generation, power stays in the same family, passed from father to son. For centuries, Thailand was a pure monarchy, ruled by all-powerful kings.

The Grand Palace, a compound of buildings built by a series of Siamese kings, is Thailand's best-known landmark.

In a constitutional monarchy, however, the power of a king or queen is limited. The government is run by and for the people. A constitution is a document that

states a country's most important
laws and values. To make sure
that no person or group gains too
much power, most constitutions
require that leaders serve only
for a certain amount of time.

A meeting of Thailand's
National Assembly

Modern Thailand has a king, a constitutional government led by a prime minister, and a National Assembly, or Parliament. The National Assembly has two parts—a Senate, whose members are appointed; and a House of Representatives, whose members are elected.

Under this system, the king has little official power, but great respect and influence. It is the king's job to look after his people, and he does that very well.

Thailand's monarch since 1946 has been King Bhumibol Adulyadej. His wife is Queen Sirikit. King Bhumibol was born in 1927 in the United States, where his father was studying medicine.

The Thai people love and respect their king and queen. They are kind and caring monarchs. King Bhumibol's picture

Royal barges during a ceremony to honor the king of Thailand (above), and King Bhumibol Adulyadej and Queen Sirikit greeting their subjects (right)

appears on Thai money. The nation's most important holiday is December 5, the king's birthday.

Religion

Buddhism is the official religion of Thailand. About 95 percent of Thailand's people practice Buddhism. This ancient tradition has greatly influenced the dress, architecture, music, holidays, and daily life of people in Thailand. Thailand also has small numbers of Muslims, Christians, Hindus, and Sikhs.

Worshipers outside the Temple of the Emerald Buddha, Thailand's most sacred religious shrine (above) and ancient statues of the Buddha at Ayuthaya Historical Park (right)

Buddhism was founded in India more than 2,500 years ago by an Indian prince named Siddhartha Gautama. Siddhartha walked away from his family's power and wealth and became a monk—a wise man and teacher. To his students, Siddhartha became known as the Buddha, meaning "the Enlightened One."

In Buddhism, there is no deity, or living god. Buddhism is concerned with removing oneself from the daily pains and sorrows of life. It teaches that suffering can be ended by giving up wealth and possessions, being peaceful, and seeking personal enlightenment, or wisdom.

A wat in Bangkok
(above) and young
Buddhist monks in the
gardens of a wat (left)

Today, Thailand has thousands
of wats—Buddhist religious cen-
ters—with statues honoring the
Buddha. Many Thai boys spend
months, or even years, living as
Buddhist monks. With shaved

Buddhist monks in prayer

heads and orange robes, they spend hours each day chanting prayers. They also meditate. Meditation is the art of sitting quietly while seeking enlightenment. Buddhist monks eat only donated food, which they collect from nearby households each morning.

Food and Culture

Thai food can be spicy or mild. But it's always interesting, combining recipes from many cultures. The basic Thai foods are fish and rice. Green curries and red curries are popular, as well as various soups and noodle dishes. The most popular seasonings in Thai dishes are

A spice stall in Bangkok (left) and fish vendors in Chiang Mai (above)

nam pla (fish sauce), garlic, ginger, chilis, lime juice, and lemongrass.

A typical Thai dinner might include soup, a spicy salad, rice, fish, and vegetables. Typically, everyone sits around a big pot of rice and several

A Thai family preparing a meal (above) and Thai women carving watermelon and other fruits into intricate shapes (right)

separate bowls of vegetables and fish or meat. Each person puts rice into a bowl and then alternates bites of rice with scoops out of the bowls.

Dessert includes a wonderful variety of fresh fruits, including papayas, mangoes, and other native fruits, plus sweets made with coconut milk. Thai children also enjoy "foreign" treats such as cookies and ice cream.

Traditional Thai music and theatrical dance are an important part of Thai culture. Young people who wish to study Thai folk music can choose from dozens of traditional flutes, gongs, and stringed instruments. These are the sounds of ancient Thailand.

Thai dancers accompanied by traditional Thai instruments

The sound of modern Thailand includes the Bangkok Symphony Orchestra, as well as Asian and Western popular music. And one of Thailand's finest classical composers and jazz musicians is none other than King Bhumibol!

Thailand is famous for its beautiful silk (above) and silverwork (right).

Pottery, ornamental silverwork, and silk cloth are among the Thai handicrafts prized around the world.

Thai Elephants

Once, elephants in Thailand were used in battle and to transport logs. Today, most Thai elephants are entertainers. They perform in shows, give rides to tourists, and march in royal parades. Elephants are intelligent animals with great memories, and they seem to enjoy being trained.

Thai elephants and their *mahouts* (trainers) start working together when both are still young. Since an elephant may live to be 60 years old, a mahout and his elephant may remain good friends for life.

Thailand's Future

Thailand is home to thousands of species of wildlife. They range in size from the giant Asian elephant to the tiny hog-nosed bat, which is the world's smallest mammal. Insects, fish, and tropical wildflowers also thrive there. And Thailand has more kinds of birds than does all of North America!

Thailand's exotic wildlife includes the great Indian hornbill (top left), the large tree nymph butterfly (top right), and the Argus grouper (right).

Like the rest of our crowded planet, however, Thailand has problems. In the cities, cars and factories create air pollution. Massive logging has led to soil

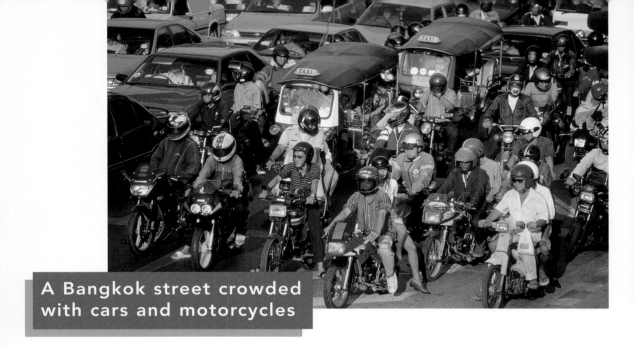

A Bangkok street crowded
with cars and motorcycles

erosion, water pollution, and
flooding. All of these harm
plants, animals, and people.

Yet in recent years, many
national parks and preserves
have been established in
Thailand. Thailand also supports
programs to protect endangered

species, stop pollution, and pre-serve its forests and seacoasts.

More and more, the Thai people are making sure that they work to save their precious natur-al resources. With continued care and cooperation, Thailand will always be The Land of Smiles.

Kao Sok National Park in southern Thailand

To Find Out More

Here are some additional resources to help you learn more about the nation of Thailand:

 **Books**

Goodman, Jim. **Thailand** (Cultures of the World). Benchmark Books, 1994.

McNair, Sylvia. **Thailand** (Enchantment of the World). Children's Press, 1998.

Thoennes, Kristin. **Thailand** (Countries of the World). Bridgestone Books, 1999.

Whyte, Harlinah. **Thailand** (Festivals of the World). Gareth Stevens Publishing, 1998.

Organizations and Online Sites

Thailand: Jewel of the Orient

http://www.pbs.org/edens/ Thailand

Based on the PBS television series, this site tells all about the history, culture, and wildlife of Thailand.

The Bangkok Post

http://www.bangkokpost. com/

Find out more about Thailand on the website of one of Thailand's best English language newspapers.

Tourism Authority of Thailand

5 World Trade Center, #3443
New York, NY 10048
http://www.tat.or.th/about/ main.htm

Good source for basic facts about geography, climate, food, population, history, religion, the monarchy, and more.

Important Words

architecture buildings

dialect variety of a language belonging to a particular region

donated given as a gift

erosion process of wearing away

exporter country that sells goods to foreign countries

minority ethnic or religious group that makes up a small part of the population

peninsula finger of land surrounded on three sides by water

shrine place or object of worship

species kind or variety of animal or plant

traditional handed down from age to age

unemployment lack of work

wisdom knowledge and the ability to use it to help oneself and others

Index

Meet the Author

David Petersen has visited much of Southeast Asia and the South Pacific. David lives on a mountain in Colorado, with elk and bears for neighbors. The author or editor of thirteen books for adults, David loves researching and writing True Books because, he says, "I always learn something new."

Photographs ©: Animals Animals: 41 bottom, 41 top right (Joyce & Frank Burek), 41 top left (E. Woods/OSF); AP/Wide World Photos: 24 (Thaksina Khaikaew), 27 bottom (Sakchai Lalit); Corbis-Bettmann: 38 right (Jack Fields), 17 top (Lindsay Hebberd), 20 bottom left (Arne Hodalic), 35 left (Wolfgang Käehler), 31 bottom, 37 (Kevin R. Morris), 2 (Charles E. Rotkin), 20 bottom right (Roman Soumar), 23 (Luca Tettoni), 19 (K.M. Westermann), 25 (Nik Wheeler), 21; International Stock Photo/Buddy Mays: 39 bottom; Liaison Agency, Inc./Elain Evrard: 1; Network Aspen/Jeffrey Aaronson: 20 top, 42; Robert Fried Photography: 11 bottom, 14 top, 29 top, 29 bottom, 34 right, 38 left; Stone: 35 right (Jerry Alexander), 12 right (Glen Allison), 34 left (Paul Chesley), 17 bottom left (Alain Evrard), 4 (David Hanson), 11 top, 43 (David Hanson), cover, 7 (Herb Schmitz), 31 top (Hugh Sitton); Viesti Collection, Inc.: 32 (Claudia Dhimitri), 6, 12 left, 27 top (Luca Tettoni), 16, 17 bottom right (Tettoni, Cassio & Associates), 14 bottom, 39 top (Joe Viesti), 17 center left. Map by Joe LeMonnier.